POSITIVE SUPPORT FOR THE GROWTH AND DEVELOPMENT OF CHILDREN WITH AUTISM SPECTRUM DISORDER

A Paraprofessionals Guide Based on Experiences with Elementary Students with ASD

Positive Hope, Positive Expectations, Positive Results

CAROLYNN A. TRUSS

ISBN 978-1-0980-2859-6 (paperback)
ISBN 978-1-0980-2860-2 (digital)

Christian Faith Publishing, Inc.
832 Park Avenue
Meadville, PA 16335
www.christianfaithpublishing.com

Printed in the United States of America

CONTENTS

ACKNOWLEDGMENTS

To my Lord and Savior Jesus Christ who blessed me with the gift of being positive and encouraging to those around me.

To my amazing son Isaac who has supported me in all my endeavors and always told me the truth in love.

To my mom who has supported me in everything all my life.

To Dr. V. Stewart for seeing in me what I didn't see in myself making this guide possible to share with others.

To Brenda Popovich for encouraging me to continue typing and writing on this project. She has been an amazing source of strength.

To Pastor Dave and Nellinda Hintz and Pastor Dean and Peggy Stewart for their moral support and encouragement.

To my team of supporters, Bob Hooper, Brandi Huff, Brenda Popovich, Laura Gualdoni, Linda Simmons, Lori Simpson, Tiffany Slates, and Susan (Fuzzy) Sanders who have been with me every step on this guide with their words of encouragement, support, and prayers.

To the parent and school support team that were the advocates for my autism training.

Thank you!

ENDORSEMENTS

This guide is an easy read loaded with Carolynn's years of experience and knowledge. I had worked with Carolynn for many years, and I could hear her voice as I read these pages. I recommend this book as a guide (not a one-time read) for all educators, pre-K through 12 grade teachers, paraprofessionals, Sunday schoolteachers, parents, and their families, to help them understand and/or teach ASD children. Thank you, Carolynn, for sharing your passion and gift with us.

Lori Simpson,
elementary special education teacher
twenty-four years

First thought was, *What a good idea!* This book contains an abundance of information and strategies to utilize when engaging with an individual on the autism spectrum. I love that it aims to increase understanding through knowledge, with the end result being improved quality of life. I love that it can be used as a go-to in time of need, and I love that it encompasses a vast audience. I have been a colleague of Carolynn's for several years now and have watched the information she is passing on *work*. I highly recommend the use of this resource for anyone engaging with an individual with autism spectrum disorder. Thank you, Carolynn, for sharing your wealth of knowledge with the community!

Brandi Huff,
occupational therapist

This guide is insightful and informative. It provides strategies for everyone who knows or works with children on the spectrum. Carolynn's passion for improving the lives of others shows through her work. Thank you, Carolynn.

Laura Gauldoni,
school social worker

Easy read, very insightful! Every educator should own as a reminder of good practice.

Tiffany Slates,
elementary special education teacher
seventeen years

GOALS OF THIS BOOK

The purpose of this book is to make your work with ASD children more understandable and manageable. The goal is to help these children have the tools they need in order to effectively learn and thrive in their classroom experience as well as other areas of their life. It is important to understand how an ASD child thinks and reacts to certain stimulation and to be compassionate and ready to give them the needed instruction so they will be able to succeed. This guide will offer suggestions in the following areas:

- Provide positive solutions to challenging behaviors. Teaching through praise.

- Teach flexibility in home, school, and their natural environment.

- Broken rules. How to handle exceptions to the rule.

- Model and pairing as a way to deal with frustration and tolerance.

- Working with the ASD mind-set.

KNOW YOUR STUDENT WELL

Interview Your ASD Child

Start your school year out positive with enthusiasm and excitement. Develop a trusting relationship with him or her.

Welcome to a new school year!

> First, middle, last, nicknames
>
> | | |
> |---|---|
> | Age | Birthday |
> | Siblings | Pets |
> | Favorite subject | Favorite treat |
>
> Hobbies: winter, spring, summer, fall

Share your *aha* moments!

Beautiful name!

I was guessing you were six years old!

My birthday is in June just like yours!

I have three brothers too!

My favorite subject is math also!

I love goldfish just like you!

Wow! Great! High five!

What Your ASD Child Likes

Knowing your student guides your intervention.

Know his or her likes and areas of interest: foods, hobbies, movies, subjects, etc. Talk about the subjects/topics and be specific.

Example of specific likes:

- Pepperoni and sausage pizza
- Hamburger with ketchup and mustard
- Strawberry ice cream
- Playing kickball, hopscotch, and basketball
- Movie "name"
- Computer game "name"
- Learning about sewing, tornados, dolphins
- Inside and outside activities (basketball, art, baseball, recess)

Wow! Awesome!

Be aware of his or her dislikes. Don't allow dislikes to be a focus.

Example of specific dislikes and your positive response to it:

- Gym, reading (*learning can be a challenge, but it helps us grow*)
- Certain foods (*my taste buds haven't adjusted to that either!*)
- Inside/outside activities (*we will do this now, but later we will do…*)

Positive! Positive! Positive!

What Upsets Your ASD Child

Understanding what upsets your ASD child may look different each time. Always expect the unexpected.

Your ASD child may have a different perception of what something should look like, sound like, or appear to be.

Example:

School pizza may not look or taste like pizza from home. That can be upsetting.

Taste bad   Look different

Reading class is over five minutes late. That can be upsetting.

Get out on time   Teach flexibility with time

It is raining at our scheduled recess time. That can be upsetting.

Have another activity choice ready: cards, drawing, blocks

A substitute teacher is coming for the day. That can be upsetting.

Use visuals to help with change.

Be prepared in advance to talk to the child about changes using an alternative prepared list.

Example: If the substitute teacher tells class to write a word twenty times (instead of the usual ten times) and the child is upset with the change, have them write it only ten times (as they usually do).

What Calms Your ASD Child

Understanding what calms your ASD child may look different each time. Always expect the unexpected! Flexibility allows you to achieve success.

Your ASD child will use different calming strategies based on the situation they are in.

Allow the child to go through the emotion and feelings they are experiencing.

Intervention:

- Take a break
- Take a walk
- Time with a friend
- Mindful breathing
- Counting
- Soft music
- Computer time
- Library time
- Mindful moment
- Time with teacher

Be prepared in advance for changes with your ASD child.

Positive! Positive! Positive!

Self-Control Strategies

Positive self-encouragement: *I can, I will, I feel.*

Quiet soft voice (low soft whisper): *I can, I will, I feel.*

- I can use my words.
- I can ask for help.
- I can take a break.
- I can count, breathe, listen to music, or take a walk.

Allow feelings to be expressed and listen to them. Understand and respect them and establish and maintain boundaries.

- Say it out loud.
- Repeat it back to me.

Visual cards are key in teaching self-control strategies. Always teach when the student is calm. That will help when the student needs to use self-control techniques.

- Relax—head down.
- Quiet time—quiet voice.
- Take a walk—walk it out/off.
- Use self-talk—encourage and affirm.
- Model self-talk—clear, cheerful, not yelling.
- *Pack up in 5, 4, 3, 2, 1* or use timer.

15

Areas of Strengths in Your ASD Child

Understanding his or her strengths will allow you to assist in their maturity ensuring they reach a greater level of success.

- Creative imagination
- Enjoys helping
- Positive attitude
- Shares with peers
- Likes to read
- Dependable and trustworthy

Encourage and allow your ASD child to enjoy and share what makes him or her successful. Awareness of their strengths will assist you in academics as well as a tool in positive behavior strategies for their success.

Positive! Positive! Positive!

Areas of Weakness in Your ASD Child

Understanding his or her weaknesses will allow you to assist in their maturity and provide positive solutions.

- Lacks organizational skills
- Lacks creativity
- Unable to make friends
- Unable to share with others
- Takes too many chances
- Takes serious situations lightly

Teach skills enabling your ASD child to become successful. Everyone has weaknesses or areas they can improve on. Awareness of those weaknesses will help you asses how you can positively assist them in these areas. Teach and model using visuals, social stories, or role-playing activities that nurture and encourage enabling your student to become successful.

Examples of using visuals:

SCHOOL EXPECTATIONS

Understanding School Rules

Be safe.

Be respectful.

Be responsible.

Be mindful.

*Review daily.

Understanding Classroom Rules

Examples of school rules:

Follow directions:

- Know direction
- Follow direction
- Read

Work quietly:

- No talking
- Whisper
- Quiet

Hands, feet, objects to self:

- Hands in pocket
- Feet on the floor
- Objects put down

Work and play safely:

- Walk
- Sit
- Play

Review daily.

Understanding Teacher Expectations

Different teacher, different expectations.

The teacher may have special signals so he or she can know what the student needs.

Examples:

    Raised hand means:
        "I have a question."
        "I have an answer."

    Pointer finder raised means:
        "I need a pencil."

    Two fingers raised means:
        "I need paper."

    Three fingers raised means:
        "I need to use the restroom."

Each schoolteacher may have a different signal system. Some schools and classrooms will have no signals. The ASD child will have to learn self-monitoring to get needs met.

Example:

    Restroom without a signal:
        Go-come back

*Review daily.

SCHOOL FUNCTIONING

Academics

Reading

Reading instructions will vary with teacher, grade level, child's reading level, and school.

ASD child may have his or her own style for reading comprehension and will need to be taught teacher and classroom expectations.

Intervention: Student is allowed to use his or her personal strategies to answer questions.

Example:

- *Teacher:* "Read the passage, then answer the questions."
- *ASD response:* "I need to read the questions first, then find the answers in the passage."

Child needs to use his or her strategies, not teacher-mandated strategies (teacher instructions).

- *Teacher:* "Underline at least one sentence in the passage that supports your answer."
- *ASD response:* "It's hard to underline a sentence. I have to circle the sentence."

They are not being disrespectful; they are communicating their needs. Child needs to do what is easy for him or her to accomplish the *task*.

Keep in mind that your child is a visual learner. Providing posters of visual instructions will be much more helpful for the ASD child than written or verbal instructions.

Writing

Writing instructions will vary with teacher, grade level, child's writing ability, and school.

ASD child may have many styles in writing unique to them individually.

- *Teacher*: "Choose one of the topics and write six sentences."
- *ASD response*: "I really don't know anything about those topics."

Child needs to choose his or her own topic to complete the assignment.

- *Teacher*: Opinion writing prompt. "What is your favorite book? Give three reasons why."
- *ASD response*: "I don't have three reasons why. I have one reason why."

Child needs to do the assignment different from the directions in order to complete the assignment either written or verbal.

Intervention: When a child does not have additional ideas, provide idea prompts for him or her.

Work to expand the students' ability within their ASD mind-set. Be mindful and patient with the process.

Positive! Positive! Positive!

Math

Math instructions will vary with teacher, grade level, child's math skill level, and school.

ASD child may have their own style for solving equations and will need to be taught teacher and classroom expectations.

Intervention: Allow your students to use their personal strategies to solve problems.

- *Teacher:* "Break apart the equation."

  10 x 4

  2 x 5 2 x 2

- *ASD response:* "Why? 10 x 4 = 40. I don't understand why I need to do extra work!"

Child needs to do what makes sense to him or her.

- *Teacher:* "Cut out the fractions at the bottom of the page. Paste them at the correct place on the number line."
- *ASD response:* "It takes too long to cut out twenty squares. I can write them on the number line."

Child needs to complete the task his or her way.

Intervention: Modification of quantity of work, 10 instead of 20.

Telling the child, "Teacher wants to see how you came up with the answer," the ASD child may not be able to do this.

Allowing an ASD student to successfully solve a problem is more important than learning a variety of problem-solving strategies. The student needs consistence, structure, and repetition.

Science

Science instructions will vary with teacher, grade level, child's ability, and school.

- *Teacher*: "Draw and label nine planets in the solar system."
- *ASD response*: "I can't do it!"

Child wants/needs assistance with the labeling.

- *Teacher*: "Copy the definitions of force and motion."
- *ASD response*: "Can I show you what the difference is? That is too much writing."

Child needs to demonstrate what the teacher is asking.

Intervention: Provide prompts to start the child's response.

Your turn/my turn.

See if the child can dictate the answer if a scribe is available.

If a student refuses or says he or she can't do something, the teacher must realize they are not being lazy or rebellious, but rather they are expressing frustration or being overwhelmed by the task.

Positive! Positive! Positive!

Social Studies

Social studies instructions will vary with teacher, grade level, child's ability, and school.

- *Teacher*: "Study the photograph of labeled artifacts, then answer the questions."
- *ASD response*: "I don't know how to study a photograph."

If child is unclear about the directions, ask specific questions to guide the student's understanding. Define words so student is clear on what it means (*artifacts: dead long ago*). Teacher must not assume the student knows and understands the vocabulary and what to do.

- *Teacher*: "Describe landforms in the state of Michigan."
- *ASD response*: "That's too much work. It's too hard for me."

Child sees an overwhelming amount of work in the assignment.

Intervention: Break assignments into smaller units. Define what it means to study a photograph. Student may not understand the word "study" in the context of looking at a picture.

Determine if the student understands. Allow time for clarity of direction. Make sure they understand.

- Clear directions
- Visual pictures
- Oral retelling
- Drawing

High five to confirm understanding!

Music

Music instructions will vary with teacher, grade level, child's ability, and school.

- *Teacher*: "Repeat the sound you hear after me."
- *ASD response*: "The sound is too fast."

The student may not be able to keep up with the beat. Work alongside of them to assist.

- *Teacher*: "There are two songs to play today."
- *ASD response*: "I can only play one song."

Child prefers to play without following directions. Two songs may be overwhelming. Praise success of one song, then work on number two.

Child may have preferences to music and instruments based on his or her tolerance of music. Loud music or noise can be over stimulating.

Intervention: If the child is sensitive to sound, he or she may need noise-reducing headphones, earplugs, or what is physically comfortable.

Role-play appropriate responses for music!

Physical Education

PE instructions will vary with teacher, grade level, child's ability, and school.

- *Teacher*: "Run relay races."
- *ASD response*: "I can't run very fast."

Child is insecure about their ability.

Child may be limited as to the activities he or she is attempting to accomplish. Allow extra time for task completion.

Intervention: Walk, run, or play alongside the child to keep him or her motivated. Give them a sense of success and guidance. Assist, but independence is the key.

- Encourage peers to assist
- Share strategies for success.

Teach proper attitude about winning and not winning.

- Great job ⟶ We played hard.
- Awesome ⟶ We will rise again.
- Fantastic ⟶ We are a great team.

Encourage your child to use strategies to assist in acknowledging outcomes on both sides, such as high five, fist bump, or handshakes. Teamwork and fun are the goals for PE class.

Student may demonstrate behavior different from expected. Refrain from asking "why." Ask them to demonstrate by saying, "Show me sitting," and "Show me quiet," during instruction in class.

Use of Technology

Technology instructions will vary with teacher, grade level, child's ability, and school.

ASD child may have one or many styles in learning using technology.

- *Chromebook*
- *Cell phone*
- *Laptop*
- *Computer*
- *iPad*
- *Smart Board*

Include your student in choosing what works best for him or her.

1) Curriculum supports may include picture lessons, student work examples, and picture of completed work.
2) Visual schedules including all classes, all subjects, all activities, and expectations during each school day. Print, post, and use daily.
3) Communication with student and parent in all areas of the school day.
4) Positive student engagement in technology such as calming, breaks, distractors, and learning support.

Example:

Teacher: "I'm going to text your mom you're having an amazing day!"

ASD response: "Can we send her two thumbs up emoji?"

Including your student gives him or her a great sense of accomplishment which keeps them encouraged and positive about their day.

Special Activities

Field Trips

Field trip instructions will vary with teacher, grade level, child's ability, and school.

- Teacher: "We are going to a play."
- *ASD response*: "I will have to sit too long."

Intervention: Child must be taught field trip expectations in great detail. Be prepared in advance to provide alternatives.

Examples:

- Time away from the activity.
- Break to the hallway.
- Stand in the back of room.

Changes of any kind can be overwhelming to an ASD child. Anything that is unfamiliar or unusual (sound, people, or activities) can cause them stress. The ASD child may be overwhelmed by sensory stimulation.

Intervention: Prepare in advance to help them through the change. Be sensitive to his or her needs. Use pictures for a visual tour of the activity so they develop a familiarity with it and are not lost or overwhelmed. Be aware of things that will stress them out and provide necessary breaks.

Encourage your ASD child using positive praise:

Good job trying new things!

Assemblies

Assembly instructions will vary with teacher, grade level, child's ability, and school.

- *Teacher*: "We are going to honors assembly in the auditorium."
- *ASD response*: "I don't want to go."

Child wants to make his or her own choice.

Intervention: Teach the child the teacher's expectations.

Overstimulation may become problematic during assemblies. The time frame with noise levels, group size, as well as activity may overwhelm them.

A visual schedule of the program will allow your child an opportunity to see and anticipate what will happen first to last. Prepare in advance!

- Teach off campus expectations (example: *movie*).
  First, then, next, last, through visuals
- Teach community expectations (example: *library*).
  First, then, next, last, through visuals

The more the child knows beforehand going into it, the more enjoyable the experience will be.

Quiet / Hands to self / First then

Key: Be prepared in advance, monitor level of toleration, and have a plan for breaks and time away.

SECTION 4

SOCIAL SKILLS

Understanding School and Classroom Rules

Teaching social skills will vary with each child. Teaching, reteaching, modeling, and role-playing will need to be put in place.

Your ASD child may have his or her own style of learning. The child's interest will be very helpful as you teach social skills.

Your ASD child must be able to communicate well with peers and other people.

- Following directions
- Listening to instructions
- Asking for help
- Being respectful
- Embracing differences
- Actively participating
- Sharing with others
- Taking turns
- Patiently waiting
- Being an encourager
- Showing good manners

Use each interaction as a teachable moment giving praise. Also praise during redirection. Encouragement will keep the child focused on the task he or she is engaging in.

Understanding School and Classroom Rules

Rule: Respect staff and peers.

Expectation: Attend school daily with positive routine and an attitude of respect.

Respectful	Patiently wait
Kindness	Encourage others
Friendly	Ask for help
Sharing	Quiet voice
Helping others	Participate equally
Good manners	Embrace differences
Polite	Say I'm sorry

Positive! Positive! Positive!

Behavior example:

Listening to announcements	Participating in the teacher's class	Sharing and helping others

Hallway

Understanding School and Classroom Rules

Hallway instructions will vary with teacher, grade level, child's ability, and school.

- *Teacher*: "Walk on the right side of the hallway with folded arms, face forward 'O' voice."
- *ASD response*: "I can't do it that way!"

Intervention: Teach and practice the "mandatory" parts of the rule.

Investing the time up front is well worth the effort.

- Right side
- Face forward
- Behind someone
- Respect personal space
- Stay in line

Allow exceptions as needed; use encouragement and praise:

Great job! Awesome job!

Restroom

Restroom instructions will vary with teacher, grade level, child's ability, and school.

- *Teacher:* "Time for restroom break."
- *ASD response:* "I refuse to use the restroom at school."

Your ASD student may not want to use the restroom at school. The noise, the stalls, and others in the restroom are very different from home.

It's very important for ASD children to learn the rules of the restroom especially boys using urinals.

Encourage him or her to use the restroom using visuals step by step.

Be flexible. Find alternative ways to use the restroom at school. It could be alone, before or after others.

Prepare in advance how you will address toileting with your student.

Be patient! Be kind! Be positive!

Praise!

Class Routine: There Will Be Changes

Prepare Students for Substitute Teachers

Teaching class routines will vary with each child. Teaching, reteaching, modeling, and role-playing will need to be taught. Review expectations.

Prepare your student in advance for a substitute teacher. This will allow him or her to understand the change for the day. Help the child to adjust to the change.

- Sub has a different teaching style.
- Sub follows teacher instructions.
- Sub will not teach like your teacher.

Your ASD child may have anxiety with a routine change. Positive encouragement will help with anxiety.

Example:

- *Wow, you are doing great with that worksheet!*
- *Great job with those math manipulatives!*
- *Those pictures of the solar system are awesome!*
- *Check out my solar system drawing!*

Have a packet ready for the substitute and prepare them for the needs of your ASD student.

Fire Drills, Lockdowns, Tornado Drills

Understanding your ASD child's tendencies will guide your intervention.

Teaching

Your ASD child may not be able to differentiate drills. Practice in advance.

- Fire drill sound
- Lockdown procedure
- Tornado drill sound

Drills may be different from school to school. Safety for all students is first. Practice all drills in preparation for the unexpected.

Strategies that are outside of the box will help accommodate the need of your ASD child.

After the drill, review what happened.

Example: Take him or her to the window after the drill showing that there is no tornado. This will give the child peace, calm, and understanding of the drill.

Videos and social stories will assist with understanding.

Socially Acceptable Words

Positive Speaking

Teach ASD students to be appropriate when he or she talks to others. Assist in replacement of *red words*. Ask the child what he or she thinks the *green word* should be.

Red	*Green*
• I *hate* you.	I *don't like it* when you do that.
• Your perfume smells *gross*.	Your perfume is *different*.
• Your color page is *ugly*.	Your color page is *interesting*.
• Your chili is *nasty*.	Your chili is *flavorful*.

Reinforce that *red words* are never to be spoken.

Other red words:

Ask child if they know what this means:

- All cuss or swear words
- All derogatory words (put-down words)
- All attacking words (bulling words)

Help child to replace all *red words* with appropriate *green words*.

Giving them an alternative will help with their social skills while letting them feel like they are still expressing themselves.

Example:

| I *hate* that. | Change to: | I *don't like* that. |
| That's *stupid*. | Change to: | That's *different*. |

Real Life

Understanding your ASD child's tendencies will guide your intervention.

Teaching Expectations

There are exceptions to the rules. Exceptions do not always have a logical reason but an emotional reason for your ASD child.

Example:

- Your ASD child will stop at a stop sign but need to be taught when it is okay to go (look both ways; don't stop in the middle of the street). *After stopping, you can go if it is safe!*
- Your ASD child will go line up in front of the grocery store line. They need to understand going to the end of the line, waiting their turn. Teach turn-taking.
- Your ASD child may have a song in his or her mind and start singing loudly at the movies. They are not aware that this might disturb others. Teach social rules in group settings (cannot sing out loud, physical boundaries, not sitting/standing without permission).

Do not assume that the ASD child is misbehaving, showing disrespect, or is willfully being lazy. Most of the time, it is just a misunderstanding, or they are simply obeying in a *literal* or *narrow sense*. Discover what the confusion is and solve problem with patience and understandable communication.

Teaching strategies in real life may be accomplished in a variety of ways. Walking, standing, or sitting alongside your ASD child using visual pictures when necessary will assist him or her as you model appropriately when exception to the rules have unexpected reasoning.

UNDERSTANDING YOUR ASD CHILD

Check on Me

I feel awesome!

I feel good!

I feel frustrated!

I feel frustrated and need help!

I am angry!
I want out!

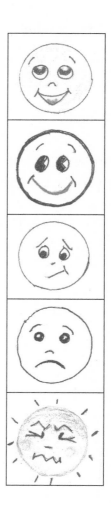

Work with ASD, Not Fighting the ASD

Understanding your ASD child's tendencies will guide your intervention.

Use your tools:

Visual schedule	School rules
Prompt/cue cards	Classroom rules
Behavior plan	Simple directions one or two words
Mindfulness	Expectations

Remember, go with the flow. Work with your student; be understanding, patient, kind, and positive.

What to expect? The unexpected!

Example:

- *Teacher*: "We are having chocolate cookies today."
- *ASD response*: Today, he or she loves chocolate. Tomorrow, he or she never eats chocolate.

Respond positively: "Okay, great. No problem."

- *Teacher*: "We are going outside for recess."
- *ASD response*: Today, he or she loves playing in the sun. Tomorrow, he or she can't go out in the sun.

Respond positively: "Wow! Great! We will play in the shade."

Personal success is under your control. Even when *they* change, *you* stay the same!

Consistency is key!

Empathy! Encouragement! Positive! Praise!

Your ASD child needs to feel they are understood. No two students are alike.

Be Aware

Your awareness of the ASD mind-set is crucial to your success.

- Be very *consistent* in your daily routine.
- Turn "it" around and make "it" work for you and your ASD student.

The "it" is whatever will lead to a successful experience in your day.

Do not take or make anything personal. The ASD mind-set may/could change without recognizable signs. They may have literal interpretation of your words or of a classmate's words and phrases (e.g., any phrases or slang expressions).

Note: These phrases will change each year.

Example:

- It's raining cats and dogs: there are no cats or dogs.
- Get out of here: it does not mean you have permission to leave.

Be supportive! Be positive! Be ready!

Quiet soft responses
Firm or direct
Whisper

Keep a Notebook to Review Success and Ideas for Improvement

Know:

- What works?
- What I need to tweak?
- What I need to stop?
- What student input I used?

Have:

- Prompts available in all subjects
- Rewards available at all times (reward in secret)
- Stickers, free time, treats, high five

Keep:

- Keep ongoing records of data relating to your ASD child in order to watch for patterns in their behavior. These patterns can change when there are changes in their life. Keeping records helps you better understand and assist your child.

Spontaneous:

Use *your* spontaneous ideas as a distraction when frustration is observed.

- Cell phone—share a video of the lesson being taught (volcanos).
- Seasons—share a video of today's weather (rain).
- Holiday—share a video of the upcoming holiday (4th of July).

Use distraction questions and statements to redirect student

Isn't the snow falling very pretty? (Awesome!)

Can you help me find my lunch bag? (Thank you!)

Isn't that a beautiful picture? (Wow!)

Did you know I have a new dog? (Yay!)

The pizza for lunch was delicious today! (Yum!)

When you observe a situation that may be problematic, use *your* judgment. *Safety first! Let's take a walk! Come with me please!*

In Your Notebook

Redirecting Your ASD Child

Say the words!

Show me: *quiet*
           sitting
           standing

Please/thank you

If they are walking/running, "freeze" rather than "stop."

The word "stop" has been used so much they ignore the word.

Please/Thank you

Give *praise notes* during each class:

- *Great job reading* (thumbs up).
- *Great job writing* (thumbs up).

Praise/positive stickers or signs

Ask the child to choose what they want from three or four choices.

Put stickers on shirt or hand.
Draw signs on papers. ♡ ☺ ☆
(Look at your "get to know me" form for ideas)

Get to Know Me

Name _____   Sisters _____
Nickname _____   Brothers _____
Birthday _____
Age _____

My Favorites

Yummy

Food _____
Fruit _____
Vegetable _____
Cake _____
Cookie _____
Snack _____
Candy _____
Dessert _____
Drink _____

I like to

Color _____
Draw _____
Write _____
Add _____
Subtract _____
Play outside _____
Video games _____

After school, I love to go.

Home _____
Movie _____
Friends _____
Park _____
Grandparents _____
Mall _____

Favorite

Book _____
Movie _____
Animal _____
Color _____
Shape _____
Travel _____

Allergy

_____
_____

Section 6

WEBSITES

www.autismspeaks.org
www.autismspeaks.org/directory
www.do2learn.com/#
www.livingwellwithautism.com
www.victoriesnautism.com

About the Illustrator

Susan "Fuzzy" Sanders is a graduate of Beecher High School, class of 1978. She loves the arts and she loves life.

About the Author

Carolynn began her start in education in 1993 as a special education paraprofessional in a preprimary impaired (PPI) classroom. She also gained experience in an emotionally impaired (EI) classroom. Carolynn has held the position as a paraprofessional in a cognitively impaired (CI) classroom, a resource room, in general education classrooms, as well as one-on-one with autistic students. Carolynn was chosen to be the chairperson of the Positive Behavior Intervention Support Team (PBIS) at her school.

In the fall of 2001, Carolynn was asked to be a one-on-one for a student with autism. Her students' parents, along with the school support team, advocated for her to be a part of the case study in which the family was chosen to be a participant for the 2001–2002 school year. This intensive training program on autism was provided by START (Statewide Autism Resources and Training) project through Grand Valley State University. This training not only provided Carolynn with additional knowledge and strategies to help students but also gave her the opportunity to train at workshops for countywide teachers and professionals with a fellow social worker, Laura Gauldoni. Carolynn has worked in six elementary schools in all grades with all ages including over fifteen students with autism. Carolynn was also awarded the Optimist of the Year award in 2005–2006. She is grateful to share what she has learned over the years.

CPSIA information can be obtained
at www.ICGtesting.com
Printed in the USA
LVHW020023310520
656910LV00006B/693